Stop

''Stop!'' said the milkman,

but the truck went on.

"Stop!" said the boy,

but the truck went on.

"Stop!" said the girl,

but the truck went on.

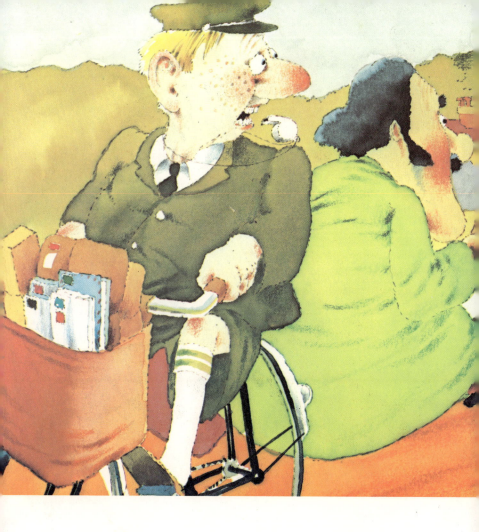

"Stop!" said the postman,

but the truck went on.

"Stop!" said the policeman,

but the truck went on.

Stop! Stop!

Stop!

"Stop!" said the traffic light.

15